Organize Yourself Starting Today!

Effective Strategies to Take Control of Your Life, Your Mind and Your Future

Copyright © 2014 by Nick Bell

Disclaimer

This document is geared towards providing exact and reliable information in regards to the topic and issue covered. The publication is sold with the idea that the publisher is not required to render accounting, officially permitted, or otherwise, qualified services. If advice is necessary, legal or professional, a practiced individual in the profession should be ordered.

- From a Declaration of Principles which was accepted and approved equally by a Committee of the American Bar Association and a Committee of Publishers and Associations.

About Me

My name is Nick Bell. Just a couple of years ago, I was one disorganized mess. I somehow never seemed to finish any projects on time, I was always late for appointments and I spent a lot of time simply trying to find things.

At one point, I spent over an hour looking for an important file, and was late for a very important meeting with a client. The project that I slaved on for several months was turned down, and that nearly cost me my career. This was a bitter turning point in my life. I realized how the little things I'd been overlooking, like being disorganized with files and stuff, had so much impact on my life and my future.

I never wanted to be in that painful situation again, and so I decided to do something about it. I researched the different techniques I could adopt to help me on my journey to becoming more organized, and this book is a compilation of strategies that I have applied to help me have a more organized life.

About This Book

This book is broken down into four different sections.

The first section looks at the importance of having an organized life. This section will give you the motivation that you need to get organized.

The next section helps you to get started on being organized by providing strategies to help you understand where the disorganization starts, in order for you to squash it quickly.

The third section provides the different strategies to get you started on being organized.

Finally, the last section provides strategies to enable you keep organized even when life around you makes you feel overwhelmed.

Please note that this book has two very important sections at the end. You will get to know how to put the information in this book into action as well as some key takeaways from this book. To help you better understand the book, here are the contents.

Table of Contents

Introduction

What are you feeling right now? Are you happy and content? Are you tired, lonely, or bored? When was the last time you had a relaxing day off? Is a day enough to tick off all the tasks on your to-do list, or do you feel like you cannot seem to get anything done on time? Are you always in a last-minute rush trying to finish your projects?

At home, do you feel restless? Are you unable to do the things that you enjoy? Don't you ever have time to relax and spend time with friends and family?

If you are experiencing these things, then it is about time that you organized your life! Most people do not realize that being disorganized not only makes it hard for them to achieve anything, but it also makes it hard for them to enjoy life.

Everyone is given the same 24 hours each day. Some people maximize this and achieve a lot. Do you make the most out of it too?

If you have a disorganized life, 24 hours seems too short to finish anything. The time between waking up and going back to bed (even at 2am!) seems like one full rush hour, with so many dangling ends to knot. Being disorganized also makes you feel like you have lost control of life and are just moving with the tide. Achieving any goals might seem like too much work – and this is dangerous.

I am sure you have dreams and goals, and have plans of the many things you want to achieve. Even though things have not turned out as you wanted them to, there is still time! There is still hope! How?

Organizing your life is the first step to achieving your goals. This is the best way for you to realize what went wrong where and make the necessary changes. This book contains strategies to help you get on your feet and organize your life, to achieve all that you ever dreamed of achieving. Best of luck to you, dear reader! I am with you every step of the way.

Chapter 1:
The Benefits of an Organized Life

Before I introduce you to the various strategies that will bring order and peace to your life, I feel that it would be better for you to have a glimpse of the many benefits of having an organized life.

You might have been thinking about fixing this part of your life, but did not have a clue on where to begin, or how to begin. This book is a great first step! It acts as a guide on how to make the first move towards the fulfillment of a stress-free and organized life. I will share the strategies which will be discussed later in this book to better organize areas in your life that need a little sprucing up.

For now, we need to motivate you to get started on having a clutter-free life; we will have a look at several benefits of being organized. You might wonder what the point of having an organized life is. You might enjoy just throwing things all over the place or not having to put in the work to get things put away at the end of the day. If you are wondering why you should choose to live an organized life, there are a lot of great benefits to doing it. Below are just some of them:

Save Money

One of the first benefits of having a more organized life is that you will be able to save money. How can you save money by being more organized? For one, think of the many times you've found yourself rummaging through your mail only to find overdue bills! Being late on the bills is going to cost you a lot of money in late fees, and just by having a more organized life, you will be able to put the bills in a place where you can find them and pay them on time, thus saving money. An organized office or home will have all the bills in one place and arranged according to which bills need to be paid first. If you do this, you will never miss a bill! On the other hand, if mail is all over the place, bills might be buried or misplaced. By the time you realize they're due it will already be too late to pay them, and you'll have to pay penalties and other fees as well. Imagine all that avoidable cost you could save if you only organized your mail.

Also, when you are organized, you can save money on daily expenses. You can plan your meals ahead of time, you can budget well, and know all the things that you need to buy at the grocery store. You won't need to make several stops because you forgot stuff. If you are able to put a list of the things that you need together before you head out, you can avoid having to go to the store every day of the week or several times in the same day. This is going to save you a lot of time, as well as the money that you would be spending on the gas to go back and forth. In addition, if you are like many people, each time you go to the store you will find something else that you would like to buy, whether or not you really need it, and you might end up purchasing it. You could save money by not going as much and not putting yourself in way of the temptation. Besides that, if you are not organized, it is very easy to buy an item only to realize that you had one already stashed somewhere at home.

Another way that being organized will save you money is that you will be able to take advantage of any of the discounts or promotions that come your way. If you want to start couponing or you get preferred customer rewards at a store that you like, organizing the paperwork for this will save you the money that you need in the long run. When papers are misplaced because you are not organized, it can end up leading to disaster and is going to mean you will miss out on a lot of the great opportunities that could be saving you money. You might also find better deals on trips and other vacations that you would like to go on. You will be able to take the time to look around at different sites, ask the right questions, bookmark the sites that you need, and get everything organized without spending more on the trip or misplacing things and having to spend extra at the last minute. There are just so many things that you will be able to save money on as long as you are able to stay as organized as possible.

These are just a few of the reasons that you will be able to save money when you live a more organized life. There are many other areas that you will be able to save money on; how much will all depend on how organized you are able to become and what areas of your life you will be able to take charge of over time.

Save Time

The next benefit of learning how to organize your life is that you will gain a lot more time. Imagine all the time you waste digging through heaps of stuff just to find your keys or credit card. Think about all of the time that you are wasting at work trying to find that report that your boss sent or get everything organized and ready to go before you are even able to start on the work that you need to do. Before I began organizing my life, there was a time I spent a whole hour looking for my car keys. I ended up being late for my doctor's appointment and that meant I had to reschedule, which was several weeks ahead! And how could I forget the missed appointment with my client that nearly cost me my entire career? Time really is gold.

With a disorganized way of life, I had hundreds of moments where I was driving to work and realized halfway there that I had forgotten something at home. So I had to go back home, spend hours on end looking for it, and then be late for work! Worse yet, I would get home and still not know where it was. You see, this was so frustrating, and added a lot to my daily stress. Many other people are dealing with these same issues all of the time simply because they are not able to keep everything in its proper place. They are wasting hours of their time just looking for the things that they need. Rather than wasting your time, you can put in a little bit of work to begin with and soon you will be able to find everything that you need without searching around. Of course it is easier to just drop things at the closest location without thinking about it than it is to make sure they are in the right place. But putting them away correctly is going to save you a lot of time and effort in the long run when you are able to find your keys or your papers instantly whenever you need them.

An organized person not only has everything they need on hand, they can also find stuff much faster. When they are looking for something, they know where it is right away and are able to go and pick it up without a problem. They are not wasting all of this time trying to find it, because they already know where it is. They are not wasting a ton of hours each week on looking for things that they need, things that are not really that important but which they need nonetheless. They are able to find what they need in just seconds and then get on with the other stuff that they have to do. The bottom line is, it is much better when you know where to find everything you need so you don't waste time trying to find stuff.

Increase Productivity

Being organized also helps you become more efficient in what you do. I also feel less stressed (and more proud) when I schedule activities and get them done on time. When you organize activities, you can weed out unimportant stuff and work more efficiently. You will be able to avoid stress, and you will feel a sense of achievement when your life becomes more manageable as well.

Think of it this way: When you get into work, what is the first thing that you spend time doing? You probably get there and have to start searching for all of the papers, emails, and other things that you need to get your project started. You might spend a lot of time searching around for the things that you need before you get started until you find them. Only once you have those things are you able to get started on the project. Then you might work for a bit and realize that you are going to need something else. If you are organized, you can just grab the new thing and get right back to work. On the other hand, if you are not organized, you are going to spend even more time just trying to find the thing that you need now. This is just more time that you are wasting without getting anything done. In addition, once you find the thing that you need, it is going to take at least a few more minutes in order to get back on track with the work, which means that even more time is wasted. Do this a couple of times and you can easily see where all of the time is going.

If you can get organized, you will be able to find everything that you need right away, which will save you money right from the beginning. You can get to work right from the start and avoid the distractions that come from spending all that time looking for things. If you do find that you are missing something and need to grab it, you can just reach right over to it and continue working, avoiding the distraction, loss of focus, and the time that it is going to take in order to find the item. This can save you hours during the day that you never realized were gone, and soon you will be getting so much more done than ever before. Think of all that free time you will have at the end of the day; you might even be able to go home on time and spend some time with your family rather than working another late night.

More importantly, all the time that you save by being organized can be used for other important things that you have always wanted to do but never seemed to have time for.

Have you been yearning to start surfing or cooking lessons, but never have the time? You may need to organize your life in order to have extra time and do more of the things that you love.

Reduce Stress

You might not have thought of this, but having a more organized life will reduce the stress that you are feeling. Most people think that being organized is more stressful and they would rather be more laid back and not have to worry about keeping things organized. This is a bad view to have. Think about it; how many times have you been stressed out because you couldn't find something when you were in a hurry and needed to get to work or to an appointment? How many times were you worried about how things would turn out at work or school because you were not able to find an important paper or something else that was needed? If you think back, there are probably quite a few times like that, and you might have had a lot of times when losing things and being disorganized was actually stressing you out more than you would think. Now think about how it would be if you were more organized in your life. You are able to find all of your papers, the keys never get lost again, and everything is exactly in the place that it should be. This does not mean that you have to get obsessive about it, but having a good system of organization in your life can make all of the difference.

There is nothing worse than the feeling of not having control over your life. This is exactly how you'll feel when you have a disorganized way of life. Can you imagine coming home to a house where the bills and the children's toys are all over the place, where even finding a place to sit is impossible? Worse still, you may move to the kitchen and find utensils and dirty dishes all over the counters.

Now, imagine walking into a nice home where everything is where it is supposed to be, and you do not end up tripping over toys all over the place. From experience, I know it feels much better and lighter when you come home to a clean and organized place. It even helps you relax!

Feel Empowered

When your life gets more organized, you will feel a surge of confidence, pride and self-esteem. Think of how great it is going to be when you can tell everyone that you got the project done on time or even early. Think of how great it is going to feel when your boss asks you for a report, or something else, and you are able to just grab it rather than telling him that you will get it back to him in a bit. Imagine how great it is going to feel when you are able to have people over because you do not have to worry about how messy your place looks. You will not even have to shy away from inviting friends to your house, because you are no longer ashamed of any mess or clutter. If you have an organized home, you will be more than happy to host guests and feel a sense of pride when they leave your home after having a great time.

All of this is going to empower you to feel so much better about yourself. Those who are disorganized might like to pretend that they are easygoing and really laid-back, but in reality, they are a big mess and might be wondering how to get everything done each day, and how others are able to remain so cool and collected. Now it is your turn to be calm and collected by getting everything in order and enjoying all that life has to offer with the feeling of empowerment.

Achieve Goals

If you want to achieve your goals, you need to eliminate the barriers that are preventing you from doing what you have to. Oftentimes, you need to streamline the different processes in your life so that you can focus your time, effort and resources on your goals. Having a cluttered way of life will make you use up more energy than is needed. This will make achieving goals much more difficult.

The benefits that you can enjoy by organizing your life are limitless! Let's start organizing!

Chapter 2:
Strategies to Get You Started
On Being Organized

Now that you know how you can benefit so much from getting organized, let's look at the strategies to get you started on your journey to being organized.

1. Evaluate Your Life

Before you can make any changes that will really stick, you need to first determine where you are right now. Truly, there must be a reason why you bought this book in the first place. Do you think that your life needs sprucing up? Are the mess and clutter weighing you down? Do you think you need help in organizing? Do you feel like you and your family will do better with an organized home?

Evaluating yourself would include an assessment of your habits, your motives (like impulse buying, for instance) and your status right now. What are the reasons that you are so disorganized in your life? Are you used to receiving papers or important things and then just tossing them aside, without paying any attention? Are you too tired at the end of the day to take the time that is needed in order to clean up your home? Do you have a lot of things that you do not need in your home? (That could indicate you are an impulse buyer and are getting a lot of things that are cluttering up your whole life.) These are just a few of the things that you will need to go over and evaluate, in order to determine why you are not as organized as you would like, so that you can eventually go through and make the right changes.

As you evaluate yourself and your life, determine what you feel about having a disorganized place, and write down some of the things that you will happily gain from being organized. It is important that you be as honest as possible with this evaluation as this will form the basis of your journey towards a more organized life.

2. Determine the Root of Your Disorganization

Once you have evaluated your life and resolved to change the status quo, you need to determine the root of the current situation, of why you are disorganized. It could simply be procrastination, not having enough time to clean up, or the inability to commit to finishing various tasks. It could also be that you are used to someone doing everything for you, so that you have never learnt how to organize stuff around the house.

Determining the root of your disorganization is really important because it is the way that you are going to be able to determine how to make changes. You might have realized that your life is disorganized and in chaos, but if you do not know the reason behind it, you are never going to be able to make the changes that are needed to turn it all around.

It is crucial that you determine why you have a disorganized life in the first place, in order to address the specific problems that are making it hard for you to organize yourself. Inability to determine the root of your problems will mean that you might fall back to your old ways of being disorganized.

3. Deal with the Root of Your Disorganization

Once you have determined what is making it hard for you to organize, you can now deal with the problem head-on. For instance, if you found out that procrastination is making it hard for you to organize your life, the first step is to make a schedule of the tasks at hand, and commit to it. Imagine the free time you will create for yourself when you finish things on time. Plan to fill this "free time" with things you love doing, to motivate you even more.

One thing that has always worked for me, concerning procrastination, is to tell myself that, however long I may want to delay doing tasks, I will still need to do them. Therefore, instead of having to wait until the very last minute when I am in a rush to do everything, I try to do it earlier, so that I can have more time to myself. If you know that you have to do a certain difficult task by the end of the day, you can start it early and get it over with.

4. Know What You Want

You cannot organize yourself if you do not even know what you want to achieve in life. You need to determine what you want, as it gives you the motivation to continue organizing even when you feel overwhelmed. Furthermore, when you know what you want, you can work around any challenges that come your way. Take the time during this process to discover the things that you would like out of life as well as the things that you would like to happen when you are doing the organization. This is going to help to keep you motivated during the process, so that you are able to keep working towards being motivated, as well as keeping the motivation going once you have started.

5. Get Your Priorities Straight

The only way that you will be in a position to say "no" to unnecessary tasks is if you have set your priorities. For instance, you can have a list of all the important tasks that you need to do on a daily, weekly and monthly basis. Once you have this list, and are resolved to stick to it, you can say that you have other prior commitments if someone wants you to do something that is not on your priority list. If you do not have a priority list, it will be very easy for someone to think that his or her matter is more urgent than yours, which means that you can easily be swayed.

This not only applies to your job, but also in your social life. If you have set 6:00 pm as your gym time, then you should stick to it. Even if friends tempt you to go out for a drink, you can say "no", as you already have a prior commitment. If you do not stick to this kind of thing, than you are not going to be able to get the results that you are looking for. A few times missing out on the priorities that you have set and it is easy to get out of the habit and go back to the way things were before. This is not something that you want to happen, because as discussed earlier, you will want to make sure that you are getting a stress-free and organized life with all of this great work.

6. Set SMART Goals

It is close to impossible to expect that you will have an organized life when you are unable to set goals. When it comes to goal setting, it is imperative that you set SMART goals. SMART means:

- Specific
- Measurable
- Achievable

- Realistic
- Timely

You may want to organize your life but be unsure where to start; hence, setting goals is important if you want to be successful. It is essential that you are specific about what you want to organize. If, for instance, your house or your office is out of order, be specific as to exactly how you want it to look afterwards. Do you simply want to have the files in order? Do you want a complete makeover instead?

Once you have set a specific goal, it is crucial to measure your performance in terms of how you are achieving the goal you have set. This is important, as it will help you know how you are doing and where you need to improve in order to achieve the goal of organization. If you do not have a way to measure the progress that you are making, then you will never know if you are achieving it. Take the time to find a way to measure your goal. You could choose to pick a date when you would like to have each room of the house organized, as well as your office. While the overall goal is that you are going to get the home and office organized, when you split it up by location and by rooms, you are able to tell how much has been done and how much more needs to be done in the process. If you do not do this, you are going to just be working in the dark and will not be able to see how much work you have done, nor how much you have left to get done. Make sure that you set up some method in order to keep track of your progress straight from the beginning.

I would also recommend that you set achievable and realistic goals. For instance, you may have a goal to clear most of your pending credit card debt in order to organize your financial life. While you want to achieve this, it is not logical to clear the debt within 3 days, unless of course you hit a lottery jackpot.

This simply goes back to setting realistic goals that you can achieve. It might take several months, so that it will be easier for you to clear it. While you are at it, set a limit to your spending or cut out the credit card use altogether, to make it much more achievable.

It is also important to set exactly when you need to have achieved a particular goal. For instance, you cannot simply say that "I will organize my life". Instead, you need to say that "I need to organize my life within two weeks", for instance. Once you have a time limit, you can easily hold yourself accountable when you realize that you have not achieved the goals you wanted to achieve. You can only tell that you are off the mark by measuring your progress.

7. Commit to Change

Making the decision to have an organized life is like making a resolution to lose weight, as both require discipline. Instead of looking for a quick fix, like the equivalent of a fad diet, you need to understand that getting an organized life is more of a lifestyle change. Once you understand that organization is a means to an end (which is a less stressful and more fulfilling life), it will be much easier for you to commit to changing your life.

You need to take the time to ensure that you are going to commit to the change. It is not enough to start out one day and say that you are going to do something without taking the time to commit to it. You can say or do anything, but that does not mean that you are going to keep with it for the long term. You could get distracted or decide that it is not worth the time and effort, and go back to the way that things have always been for you. This is certainly an option, but you are not reading this book because you want things to go back to the way that they have always been. You want things to change for the better, to be something new, to get rid of the clutter that is in your life and to see how amazing it can all be for you. If this is what you want, then you need to make the commitment to the change now and stick with it.

8. Get Some Inspiration

Motivation and inspiration could be all that you need to get you started on your journey to getting organized. Making changes is very difficult. Therefore, if you are to emerge successful, you need to find a way of being continually motivated to change. If you want to stick to your resolve to organize your life, you need inspiration.

Inspiration can come from different places. For instance, you can imagine how great your life would be and all the time you would have to yourself by simply organizing. You can also look to a friend or family member who has managed to organize their life, and just imagine how much easier things are for them. You can also think of how things are bad right now, and how you have been unable to manage your life properly because of not being organized.

In any case, what do you have to lose by being organized? Actually, you have everything to lose if you do not organize your life.

9. Inform People around You of Your Decision to Stay Organized

The mistake that most people make is to assume that they can get organized without the help of those closest to them. If your close friends and family members are not aware of your decision to organize yourself, they are likely to do things that might sabotage your efforts. Therefore, it is always advisable to inform the people closest to you of this decision. Once you inform someone, it is very easy for you to be accountable to them. Furthermore, if they come to your house and find it in a mess, they will want to know what happened and maybe help you out a bit.

In any case, once you inform someone that you want to do something, you will always feel that you have let them down if you do not hold your end of the bargain, which means that you are motivated even more to do everything possible to achieve your goals. Your friends and family members could also be a source of great ideas and information which can come in handy in organizing your life.

10. Buddy Up

Trying to organize your life alone just won't cut it. While you can inform your friends and family members of your resolve, they may not understand where you are coming from, especially when they have not gone through a similar process. This is why it is important to get a friend with similar goals, with whom you can work to better your lives.

When you have a friend who understands how hard it is to say no, and how this has led to your taking on more tasks than you can handle, it becomes easier for your friend to help you out, especially since they may be struggling with the same thing. Furthermore, it will be easier to talk with such a friend. They will understand you, and may even offer you tips on getting things done much more easily. You need to understand that social support is very important for any changes you are to make in your life.

This is often the best advice that you are going to get, regardless of who you are talking to or what activity you are participating in. The more that you are able to get support, and have someone who is going to back you up along the way, the easier the whole process is going to be. You can find someone who has decided that they want to start organizing their lives at the same time as you. You can both be there to offer tips and suggestions to make things easier on each other, to make sure that the other is not falling behind, and to offer support when it seems like it would be easier to just throw things all around again. If you are not able to find a friend who is in the process of reorganizing their life, it might be possible to find someone who has already gone through this whole process. You can ask them to be your buddy and they will be able to give you words of inspiration, offer suggestions on how to make the process easier, and help you to keep going when it seems hard. Make sure that you find someone who is going to be this center of support for you when you begin, because it is going to be difficult and hard at the beginning. Fortunately, with a little bit of hard work and a good buddy to support you, it is possible for you to do it all with no issues.

11. Enhance Your Brain for Focus

Once you make a decision to organize yourself, it is important that you focus. In order to achieve this, you need to ensure that your brain operates optimally. If you feel distracted, tired and stressed, part of your brain (the prefrontal cortex) will not do its job. You can ensure that your brain has enough energy by eating well, exercising and getting enough sleep. Exercise enhances the flow of blood to the brain and nutrition ensures that your brain has enough energy from the protein, carbs and fats. Doing this will ensure that you have a focused brain.

Getting your mind to work the way that you want it to, in order to get going on the organization, can sometimes be a little bit difficult. You will want to learn how to stay focused and get the right brainwaves to be positive through this process. This is going to be a hard process to start, because you are going to have to retrain the way that you have been thinking and working for a long period of time. You are going to have to change the way that you have been doing things, and this is not something that is just going to happen for you. But with the right kind of focus, and maybe adding in a little bit of meditation to your routine, you will be able to get your mind on the right track that you need in order to get the organization to happen in your life.

Chapter 3:
Strategies to Get You Organized

12. Have a Morning Routine

How you start your day determines how it will be. If you start by waking up late, then having to rush out of the door without even having breakfast, you are likely to forget to bring important documents to work. Then you end up being late for a morning meeting, and your day is likely to be full of chaos. If you wake up late every day and have hectic mornings, this is likely to lead to a disorganized and highly stressful life, as you might never have the time to do simple things like making your bed and leaving your house in order when you go to the office. By the time you reach home at night, you'll be too tired to do anything. The worst part is, the cycle continues again the next day.

It is imperative that you develop a healthy morning routine, as how you start your day determines whether you will have a successful day. I would suggest that you learn to wake up early each day so that you have enough time to do all the important tasks that need to be done in the morning. When you wake up early, you will be in a position to go to work early, prepare well, and start working on time. You will also be in a position to plan for your day at the office, which means that you will move from one activity to the next easily.

The routine that you do is completely up to you. You do not have to follow the routine that someone else does, or one that you have heard is the best. Each person is going to be doing things in a different way and each person is going to wake up in a different way, so it does not make sense for you to go and do things in the exact same way that someone else might be doing them. If you like to get up and take a moment to read the paper with some cereal, that is fine. On the other hand, if you like to get ready by playing some happy music, getting dressed, and dancing around then this is the way that you should do the routine. As long as it is getting you up and ready to face the morning and do things in the right way.

13. Feed Your Mind with the Right Information

It is important for you to be positive about life rather than always looking on the negative side. Having a positive outlook on life is not easy – it requires hard work. A great way to ensure that you always see the positive side of life is by feeding your mind with the right things.

For starters, I would not suggest that you watch the news as soon as you wake up. This is because 80% of what's on the news will be negative.

I know that it has become a habit for many of us to watch the morning news, but perhaps you could find an alternative. Why not watch your favorite lifestyle, cooking, or music channel? Or why not spend some time meditating, reflecting or reading a motivational book. You will achieve greater peace of mind and be in a position to organize your life much better.

14. Exercise Daily

Exercise is good for you as it gives you the energy to tackle the day. When I talk about exercising, I do not mean that you have to spend several hours at the gym, just doing some physical activity to get you ready for the day. For instance, you can jog, run or do some yoga or aerobics. You will discover that exercising makes you feel much better. Furthermore, exercising gives you enough energy for the day so you won't feel sluggish. You will also be more ready to handle all the challenges for that day.

It is easy to forget to do the exercise that your body needs during the day. You might have a million other things that you need to get done, or just be too tired to deal with it all. This is the excuse that many people come up with, but it is important that you stop putting it off and instead schedule it into your day even if it means missing out on other things. The exercise that you get will help to keep your body in good shape, can help to improve your mood, and will give you the energy that is needed in order to finish some of the other tasks. This means that you might still be able to get all of your tasks done, even with the exercise, and it is a time that you can spend on your own without any obligations to other people. Even if you are only able to get away to do 30 minutes of exercise on some days, this is better than nothing and you should make sure that you are doing this as much as possible.

15. Get Enough Sleep

We all know that when we don't get enough sleep, we tend to be grumpy, moody and ready to snap at anyone at any time. Lack of sleep also affects how you function, and if you are not in the right state of mind, it becomes very difficult for you to be orderly.

I would suggest that you get between 6-8 hours of sleep each day. When you get enough sleep, you are more likely to be jovial and have enough energy to do things. This makes it easier to undertake the necessary changes to organize your life.

Sleep is one thing that a lot of Americans have difficulties with. They might have to get up early for a meeting, stay late at work, run around with their children each day to activities, meet up with friends, clean the house, etc. These activities can easily eat up your time and make it difficult for you to get to bed soon enough and stay there long enough. In addition, many people find that even when they are able to get to bed at the right time, they are not able to turn off their minds. They might be thinking about all of the things that went on during the day. Many people even have a television in their room that could be keeping them up or making it difficult for them to get a good night's sleep.

If you want to make a difference in your life and become more organized, then you are going to need to make sure that you are getting as much sleep as you can. Cut down on all of the activities that you are doing, ask for help, find ways to quiet down your mind right before bed, and make sure to turn off the TV. Do whatever it takes to make sure that you will be getting to bed at a decent time in order to get enough sleep and feel rejuvenated to begin again the next day.

16. Have a To-Do List

Once you have thought of all the tasks that you need to undertake for the day (or the week), you can then come up with a to-do list prioritized according to how important each task is. Having a to-do list is important as it enables you to remain focused on what needs to be done, when and where. This enables you to stick to your plans and not change them, because you know that if you do not do a particular task at a certain time, it will push the other tasks further from completion, and you will have a series of tasks waiting to be completed all at the same time. Trust me, ask around and you will find that all people who have managed to organize their lives have a to-do list.

When you are making your to-do list, take the time to write out all of the things that you think you need to get done during the day. This is the time that you should write out as many details as you are able to, in order to make sure that nothing is left out. You will be able to cut things out later on, but this is a good place to start. When you have a to-do list available, you are going to be able to see what all needs to be done, you can clear out your head so that you are not thinking about these things all of the time, and then you will be able to check things off and see your progress as you go along. Before you go to bed each night, it is a good idea for you to write out your to do-list for the next day, so that you can clear out your head before bedtime and be ready to go right away in the morning.

17. Make Your To-Do List Brief

Ensure that your to-do list is as brief as possible. If you have a long list of things, your mind feels overwhelmed and already starts resisting what you plan to do. To avoid this scenario, you can have five tasks on one index card, for instance, and then have the other items on another card. That way you will not feel overwhelmed that there is so much to do such that you are tempted to give up altogether.

Make sure that you are only putting the things that you really need to get done on the to-do list. Little things that are not that important can wait until later. A brief to-do list is much better because it lets your mind take a break from thinking and makes the tasks seem more manageable. If you do have a lot of things to do, it is fine to start out with just a few of them, get them done, and then start on a new to-do list later on once you've cleared the first one. This will ensure you get things done, but it breaks them into more manageable chunks for you.

18. Divide and Categorize the Different Tasks that Need to be Done

It is very easy to waste a lot of time moving up and down trying to organize your home. The same is true with going back and forth between your desk and filing cabinet at work. It is advisable that you categorize all the tasks that need to be done, so that you can spend less time searching for them and more time finishing them.

For instance, when you have decided to organize your clothes cabinet, you can do many different things at once. You can separate the clothes (shoes, bags, belts, coats, etc.) that you often use and don't use anymore, those that fit and those that don't. Then you categorize the ones you don't use and don't fit into those that you can sell, give away or dispose of. This makes your work easier and more productive, as you can finish different tasks all at once. At the end of the day, you have a cleaner cabinet and maybe even have a few dollars from the clothes you've sold.

This categorization of tasks will ensure that work flows seamlessly.

19. Make Schedules and Have Deadlines for All Your Goals

One thing that I am certain of is that organized people don't waste time. They see the need to keep things organized if they expect to be really productive. This means that you need to make schedules, not only for the day but also for the week or month ahead. After that, make deadlines for set goals and schedules, and ensure that you stick to those goals.

If you live a cluttered life, you are unlikely to be in a position to achieve your goals, which means that you will always be behind with work. A great way to get you going in terms of setting schedules and deadlines is to write down the things you want to achieve in your life today, this week and this year, then come up with strategies on how you are going to achieve whatever you have written down. Set a deadline for when you need to have achieved those goals and work towards meeting them within the set deadlines. Write the plan. Post it on your refrigerator door or vanity mirror. Practicing this will help you check on yourself often, and to be on your toes to achieve your targets.

20. Always Stick to Your Schedule

Once you have come up with a plan and set a deadline for it, be honest with yourself and stick to your schedule. Never make any excuses. It makes no sense to use a lot of time developing a schedule only to forego it – that would just mean more wasted time.

Organizing your life is all about making plans and sticking to those plans. If you had planned to organize your house on Saturday afternoon between 3 and 4, stick to that, even when a friend invites you over for coffee (if you go for coffee, you will not do the task; that means that you will end up having to do it next Saturday and forego other plans for that day). If you really want to spend some time with your friend, why not set a date and put that into your schedule. It's all about making wise trade-offs.

Of course, there are going to be times when you have something that is going to come up and change the things that you are trying to do. These occasions are a part of life that you are just going to have to deal with. When they happen you will have to veer from your schedule a little bit in order to make things work out the best that you can. But try to keep things as normal as possible so that you are able to get everything done and still stay as organized as possible. It is good to have some flexibility in your life, but do not become so flexible that you are avoiding the things that you need to do to stay organized.

21. Do Not Dwell

It is important to prioritize tasks according to how important or urgent they are. This will enable you to avoid messy instances of having too many things to do at one time. However, even as you prioritize tasks, it is important not to dwell too much on one thing. You need to understand that a day has only 24 hours, and if you are unable to complete daily tasks, you will automatically start another day piled up with too many things to do. I would suggest that you set a time limit for each task that you want to accomplish. You will need to focus on it to be able to finish as much of it as you can. Once the time is over, move on to the next task. At the end of the day, you can go back to the tasks for which you ran out of time. Dwelling too much on one task can be counterproductive. Your brain also benefits from breaks, as switching to other tasks for a while becomes a breather.

The most common reasons that people have for dwelling too much on a task are that the task is too difficult or the resources to do it are not available. For instance, the simple task of trying to get a stain off your sink can take too long. Instead of slaving over it for many hours to get it right, why not ask for help? If you ask for help early enough, you will be assisted and you won't have to waste so much time. If you need assistance with organizing different places in the house, ask for help early enough so that you do not dwell too much on one task and ignore other equally important tasks.

22. Be Methodical About Organizing

Once you make a decision to organize your life, you need to figure out the areas of your life that are in most need of organization. It could be your office, your house or home office. Once you decide where you want to start, divide the organizational process into small, bite-sized projects with a clear strategy on how to complete them. This methodical approach will ensure that you do not miss anything in the process.

Having some method to your madness is one of the best ways to make sure that things get done. You should make sure to have a plan in place before beginning. What are your overall goals for this whole process? This is the first thing that you are going to need to figure out in order to get started. Now you will have to take the time to figure out all of the steps that need to be taken in order to reach the overall goal. If you are looking to become more organized in your life, you might separate it into the different rooms of your home or places in your office. You can then set up a method to follow in order to get each of the locations organized so that you can get the best results. This is going to take some time, but you will be really happy with the results in the end.

23. Create Outlines for Your Goals

While setting goals and establishing schedules and deadlines are great, it is equally important to have an outline of all the things that you want to achieve. For instance, if you want to organize your business so that you can respond to customer queries faster and deliver goods to customers more quickly, you'll need to have an outline to show the procedures and the processes that you're going to follow in order to achieve your targets in one quick glance.

An outline makes it easier for you to get briefed on the day's task. It is similar to a to-do list, only it is much briefer and shows processes. For example, if you want to shop at the grocery store and do not want to get tempted into buying stuff you don't need, make an outline of the grocery run. You can make a mental map and plot which items you need to buy first, then the next, and so on and so forth. You'll need to write down the sections as well, in order for you to be more efficient. Now, if you shop at a grocery store often, you can map out the store in your head, right? You know which sections are close to each other. For instance, you could write on your outline poultry and beef (meat section) – eggs and yogurt (dairy section) – apples, bananas and figs (fruit section) – carrots, potatoes (vegetable section), etc. This way, you get to buy everything you need much quicker, without having to go around all the aisles and eventually purchasing stuff you really do not need.

If you want to organize your home office, it is imperative that you come up with an outline for what you want to achieve, according to importance.

Your outline of the day could be something like this:

- Respond to emails (work projects / weekend charity) (8am – 9am)
- Meet clients (9am – 11am)
- Finish Project ABC (3pm)
- Clear office table (5pm)

This is just a sample of how you can outline all the activities that you need to do. Once you have an outline, you can then go into each individual item in the outline and strategize how you can finish that particular task efficiently.

24. Write Everything Down

Given your hectic work schedule and busy social and family life, trying to remember everything is impossible. Even if you have a superb memory, there will definitely be some things that you will forget if you do not keep track of everything in writing. Trying to remember important dates or appointments in your head will only lead to disaster! I suggest that you start writing things down – not only to be safe, but to get more organized.

Start writing things down in a small notebook you can keep in your pocket or purse. Or better yet, put it on your smartphone (there are lots of apps for that). You will have a much easier time remembering things like birthdays, appointments, important dates, agendas for meetings, and other crucial information. Noting down everything, even the small details, will ensure that you get a more organized life. Start practicing by writing down people's names shortly after meeting them (when they are not looking of course). Trust me, you will remember names much easier that way.

25. Do One Thing at a Time

In our society, we are always on the move. We always try to do several things at the same time, and are mighty proud of it. CEOs, engineers, teachers and nurses do it. Moms, teenagers, and even kids do it too! Multitasking has gained prominence in the recent past and has even become a requirement in job applications.

However, I think that in order to be efficient, you need to focus, which is contrary to what multitasking involves. My argument is that multitasking may be more of a foe than a friend, as it reduces your ability to give something your full attention.

One study found that multitasking actually decreases your productivity, since your brain has to go through a recall process in order to determine where exactly you left off a task. Imagine all the time that your brain has to recall; how much time and focus do you think you have lost? It is important that you learn how to do one thing at a time and learn to live in the moment. This also greatly helps when you are starting to reorganize your home, your habits, and your life.

Wouldn't it be better to have completed five out of eight tasks at the end of the day, as compared to having started all the eight tasks but not having completed any of them? You'll be left with loose ends, and that will overwhelm you when you go about dealing with them again the next day.

What you should do is to prioritize and concentrate. Once you learn how to concentrate on one task, finish it and move on to the next. You will have an easier time organizing since you will not have too many tasks at the end of the day.

26. Use the Pareto Principle to Organize Your Life

If you are not familiar with the Pareto Principle or the 80-20 Rule, start learning and using it today, as it could come in handy in helping you achieve your goals. The Pareto Principle is that 20 percent of input is likely to yield 80 percent of the result. This means that at the workplace, only 20% of the workers will produce 80% of the results. Or that 80% of your sales come from 20% of your clients. Simply put, things should be maximized in order to get the most benefits. You should know where or what the 20% is, in order for you to focus on it to yield greater results – like rewarding the 20% of workers, or the 20% of clients, instead of spending resources equally on all workers and all clients.

Using the same principle in organizing your life, realize that 20% of the efforts you put towards making a better life for yourself yield 80% of the results. This means that not everything you do will yield the 100% output in terms of having a better life. Your goal is to figure out what this 20% is in order to use the Pareto Principle to your benefit. Once you know what the 20% stands for, you can then align your life appropriately and not have to do so many things that don't add much value or contribute heavily to achieving your goals of having an organized life and a better future.

27. Don't Make Snap Decisions

I know that there are instances where we have to make decisions on the spot. But unless it is an emergency, it is important that you think through different things before making a decision. It is very easy to take on responsibilities before you even sit down and think if you are able to handle these responsibilities.

Once a person asks you to do something that needs to be done, it is important that you take your time first to evaluate the commitments you currently have before taking on a new one. This will ensure that you will not have to postpone doing your things to do other people's things. Your goals should be the priority, not other people's plans.

28. Set Time Limits for Making Decisions

Although I discourage you from making snap decisions, I also disagree with taking too long to make a decision. Some time back, I really struggled with making very simple decisions like what I would wear for the day, or what I would eat for dinner. This led to me wasting a lot of time. My inability to make a decision on what to wear the night before, for instance, would mean that I would waste 20 minutes every morning trying to decide on my outfit for the day.

However, once I started setting a time limit for when I had to make a decision, things changed. Now I only have to decide what to wear before I go to bed, and stick to that decision the next morning without hesitation. Once you set time limits for decisions you have to make, it becomes much easier to get things done.

29. Embrace Saying "NO"

You need to realize that even the kindest people say no. Saying "NO" does not mean that you are uncaring, but that there is only so much you can do as an individual, and at that particular moment, you are in no position to do a certain task.

I know as human beings we are wired to always answer in the affirmative; however, learning to say "no" to certain tasks is important if you want to have an organized and stress-free life. If you keep on reassuring people that you can do different things all at once, you will get your plate full, and you will lose precious time for your own tasks. The only way to have an organized life is taking on what you know you can do and saying "no" to unimportant tasks that you are unable to undertake. Again, stick to your plans and schedule.

30. Give Everything a Home

It is very easy for things to get lost when they do not have a specific place where you put them. Organizing means keeping things in their proper places. A great tip to help you get started is to always ensure that you create easy-access storage spaces for things that you use frequently. For instance, you can have a pen holder to put your pens, pencils and frequently used stationery. Since you are likely to be using these items frequently at your office, store them in a place that you can access easily. Also, ensure that you do not let your storage spaces become cluttered. Always find new ways of getting things from where you need them easily.

You may be tempted to label a particular storage space as miscellaneous. This is a complete NO-NO because you are likely to be tempted to dump everything that you don't use and don't want in there, and in a short time you will have accumulated clutter. Again, for things that you do not really use, give them away, sell them or just dispose of them.

31. Label Everything

This is especially important for storage boxes as well as cabinets for storing certain things. For instance, have them labeled "Game Equipment", "AC Chargers" "Receipts/Warranty Cards" etc. If you want to store books in cabinets, ensure that you label the cabinets appropriately depending with what you are storing. If it is bills and other important mail, ensure that you have a box or large folder clearly labeled as containing bills and other essential documents.

Labeling everything makes it easier for you to know where everything is. Imagine if you just put all your books in one place without really knowing the kind of books that are in a particular cabinet or box; if you wanted to get a particular book, you would really have a hard time trying to locate it. You don't need to label boxes only, you can also label where you put drugs in your bathroom cabinet as well as foods in your pantry. Learn to label almost anything that can be labeled to make it much easier to locate things. Useful tip: buy storage cases that are transparent, so it will be much easier for you to see what's on the inside.

32. Get Rid of Clutter

Clutter is simply anything that you do not need. Clutter can be physical things, like broken appliances that you keep in the garage, hoping one day to resurrect them. It could be tons of old clothes and shoes that you have outgrown but refuse to dispose of. It could also be too many electronic gadgets that you do not use (or do use but not in the most productive sense). It could be financial clutter, like too much debt from too many credit cards. All in all, clutter ultimately deters you from having a productive and tranquil life.

You need to determine what is important in your life, and get rid of anything that is taking your attention away from that. For instance, if you have too many cars, gadgets or commitments, you will need to spend a lot of time taking care of them. There is nothing wrong with having material possessions; it's only when these materials things take away precious time that you could have used to bond with family or organize your home that they become detrimental.

When you get rid of clutter, you free up space and you get more time to plan for more enjoyable stuff. Planning is usually very crucial to having an organized life because you can plan when to do certain tasks, when to pay your bills, when to clean and organize your home, when to do important and less important tasks and so on. This cannot happen if you are always in a frenzy of doing so many things at once.

33. Know Where You Can Discard Items

Organized people find time to declutter regularly, and find it therapeutic. In order to organize items, and get rid of clutter, you need to know where you should discard such items. If you don't know what to do with the items, you are most likely going to have clutter accumulate again, and all your hard work of trying to organize the house will come to naught.

You can decide to donate items to thrift stores or sell them on Amazon, eBay or Craigslist. You could also decide to donate them to charity or take them to a recycling center. You could have a garage sale and get some extra money from the sale of different items. Once you know how to discard different items, getting rid of clutter will be much easier.

34. Schedule a Major Decluttering

While decluttering on a regular basis is advisable, you need to set time aside to do a major decluttering at least twice a year, ideally before winter and after spring. In order to ensure that you don't forget your yearly decluttering, you can schedule the session, for instance, during the start or end of the school year or on someone's birthday. Just make it a time that you won't forget and are likely to have a few days free. This will ensure that things do not get out of control, since we have the tendency to buy stuff that we end up not using after a few months.

35. Don't Bring in More Unnecessary Items

Now that you have gotten rid of the things that you don't need and are already organizing your life, don't let all that hard work go to waste by bringing unnecessary things back into your home.

I would suggest that you avoid bargains and big sales, as you may find items being sold at very low prices, and the temptation to buy them, even if you don't need them, may be too hard for you to resist. I would recommend that if you want to buy something you should get rid of an item in your house to create space for whatever you think you need. Additionally, before buying anything, give yourself at least a few days to contemplate if you really need the item. Only buy that item if you still need it after thinking about it for several days.

Some important techniques that have always worked for me to ensure that I don't bring unnecessary items into the house to avoid creating more clutter are:

- When shopping, I always ask myself where the particular item that I want to buy will go (i.e., Do I have space for the item?)
- I always have a list of what I want to buy, and I try as much as possible to stick to that list.
- I always consider the money that I would save by avoiding buying that item. Even though you may think that you are making a bargain purchase, if you never even use it it's just a waste of money.
- I only bring cash when I go shopping, and leave my credit cards at home (this was painful for a shopaholic like me, but it had to be done).

36. Create a "Launch Pad" Near the Front Door

Having a launch pad next to the door is very important. This area should have all the things that you need every time you leave the house, like school backpacks, keys, scarves and umbrellas. Basically, you should put everything that you usually grab as you walk out of the door here. You can use pegs, containers and hat stands, or hooks to hold the different items.

As you enter the house, the launch pad acts like a place where you can put everything you have walked into the house with, and distribute the different things into the appropriate rooms from there. This will ensure that you do not end up carrying your keys all over the house and then not know where they are when you want to leave.

37. Have a Dump Zone

Clutter begins from the moment you step into your house. Therefore, if you want to keep clutter from accumulating, you need to have a strategy of dealing with everything. What has always worked for me is having a dump zone to put everything that I may not have the time to put away immediately, which I empty every weekend.

This is not like the launch pad. A launch pad is where you put things immediately after you enter the house, whereas the dump zone is where you temporarily dump things that might need more time for sorting. The dump zone should not be at the entry point, as this could look unsightly.

The good thing about having a dump zone is that once you have the time to get organized you don't have to walk all over the house looking for something, because you know where to find it. Furthermore, having a dump zone ensures that you do not take clutter to other parts of the house.

38. Get Rid of Financial Clutter

Understand that you also need to get rid of financial clutter. You could start by getting rid of all those 10+ credit cards that you have. Having too many credit cards is in itself clutter, because each time you need to go out and buy something, you need to figure out which card you want to carry. It is also very hard to track your expenditures when you have too many credit cards, and this brings a lot of confusion, especially when you end up spending more than you had intended and then have to sacrifice a lot to deal with those expenditures. Furthermore, having too many credit cards may deter you from doing other important tasks, especially when you want to do your own reconciliations.

I would suggest that you dispose of most of your credit cards and have one or two at most, to be used only for emergency expenses. This will ensure that you will not have to spend a lot of time tracking your expenditures on all your cards. Instead, you can use that time to do tasks that are more important.

Starting to pay off your debts is also a great way to rid yourself of financial clutter. If you want to take control of your future, you need to have it debt free. You can start by paying off one credit card at a time, closing the account permanently, and then committing to close the others sequentially. (However, do not forget that you should still pay the monthly bills on all your credit cards!) This reduces the amount of debt you have, and will slowly enable you start making better plans for your future.

39. Have a Budget for Everything

Not having a budget is recipe for failure and a disorganized life. A budget is crucial as it enables you to clearly outline how you are going to spend every single dollar you earn. Furthermore, knowing how much you spend on every item gives you some sense of order and control. If you have no budget, I am sure you feel your life is disorganized when you don't even know where your money went at the end of the month. You simply find out that you are running out of cash but cannot really account for how you spent your money.

Rather than living a life where you have so little control over your money, embrace budgeting. You will feel much more in control, and when you can see where all your money is going, you can make adjustments as you see fit. I usually have a general rule on my monthly budget: 50% on essentials (food, gas, clothing, etc.), 20% on bills, 15% on savings, 10% nonessentials, and 5% for emergency expenditures (which goes to savings if unused for the month).

40. Have a Saving Plan

If you currently don't have a saving plan, then you are headed for destruction. For starters, you should have an emergency fund that should be equal to at least 3 to 6 months of expenditures. This is your security blanket, as you never know what can happen a day or two from now. You need to understand that this is not your savings per se, but is an emergency fund in case of sudden loss of a job or other emergencies. You also need to be saving for you and your family's future. It could be a savings plan for your children's college, summer vacation, or a down payment for buying your dream house or property.

If you want to retire early, you also need to start saving early and making investments appropriately rather than simply spending all your money on short-term things that will not help your future. If you are not saving, now is the time to start. It is never too late! Know that you will feel amazing when you know that you are in charge of your life and are making financial decisions that will ensure you have a prosperous future.

41. Have Insurance Coverage

The future is very uncertain and we don't know what it holds for us. One way of ensuring that you are well prepared for uncertainties is to have insurance coverage for different things. The variety of insurance coverage you can have is almost limitless. It is therefore up to you to determine what is most important to you and ensure that you get coverage for it.

For instance, it is imperative that you have a comprehensive car insurance to make sure that you are well covered in case of theft or accident and you would not have to worry about money if something happened to your car.

It is also important to have homeowner's insurance. This will vary depending on the risks that your house may be faced with. If you live in an area that is prone to flooding, you should ensure that you have flood insurance. The thing is to simply evaluate the risks that you are likely to be faced with and make sure that you are adequately covered. You will be happier and less stressed when you know you have taken the necessary steps to ensure that certain things don't destabilize your future.

42. Process Your Mail Weekly

This applies to both physical mail and electronic mail. If you receive a lot of mail daily, you can process this daily. However, the most suitable schedule is to process it weekly. This will ensure that you do not feel overwhelmed when you see your mail piling up.

When you process your mail weekly or at least frequently, you can easily know when your bills are due and you can throw out junk mail immediately without letting it pile up. Additionally, assess the mail and emails you receive on a frequent basis. Are these very important, or are they just marketing materials? Are majority of these magazines and digests that you could check online? If so, why not forego the physical magazines and opt for a more environmentally friendly digital copy? If you often receive spam mail, check the option for unsubscribing. Trust me, your inbox will look much more streamlined when you have done so.

43. Go Paperless

Technology is simply amazing. Now you can capture almost everything and store it on your desktop, laptop or cloud. If you have too many papers and documents such as receipts, photos, and invoices, you can consider scanning them and saving them on your PC. Imagine of all the papers you will discard (and the extra storage space you'll get!) by simply learning to save things electronically. You can then use the storage space for more important things.

Once you have scanned all the documents, don't create clutter on your computer by storing everything all over the place. Once you have saved the files, sort them out in a systematic filing system (organized folders with proper labels) so that you can know where you have saved every document for easy retrieval. For example, save all the receipts in a folder named "Receipts" and you can have several folders inside for each type, e.g., tax receipts, insurance, mortgage, etc.

44. Get Rid of Toxic People

Friends are great as they encourage you to achieve your goals as well as challenge you to become better. However, not all friends are this good. Some friends can be toxic since they actually take you away from what you want to achieve.

For instance, if you make plans to organize your life and some friends start telling that you are just wasting your time, you need to seriously reconsider the kind of people around you. There is nothing worse than trying to make a better life for yourself when you are facing opposition, even from your friends who you expect to support you. The opposition will simply wear you down and, in no time, you are likely to go back to your disorganized self and be frustrated that you did not achieve your goals. Do not let toxic people rule you. Decide for yourself, surround yourself with positive people, and pursue your goals.

45. Learn to Delegate Responsibilities

Are you the kind of person who feels that no one can do anything better than you can? If you are such a person, I am sure that you are living a very stressful life. Doing everything alone is very difficult. This takes time away from yourself, and you will barely have time to organize your life. You cannot be a jack-of-all-trades. You need to learn how to delegate some responsibilities if you are going to organize your life.

You can start by going through your to-do list and removing the items that you can easily delegate to someone else. You will feel a lot better and have more time for your own tasks. For instance, if you are at work and you feel overwhelmed by all the things you need to do, you can delegate some of that work to your juniors. The work will get done on time and your boss will be happy. Better still, if your subordinates do not know how to do your work, train them so that they can work on these tasks when you are not available. This takes some stuff off your plate and at the same time, you are empowering and motivating the people under you.

If you are organizing your home, you can start by delegating some duties to your children. For instance, rather than making your children's beds every morning, why not teach them how to make their own beds? You could also ask help in preparing meals, like mixing ingredients or setting up the table. This way, you are cutting the amount of time for meal prep, and teaching your children to be responsible as well.

46. Have Some Time Alone

It is important that you learn to have your "me" time every day so that you can think about how your life is, as well as make any changes you need in order to make your life better. It is during this "alone" time that you can evaluate if you are taking steps in the right direction.

If you do not take this time, you will not be able to plan well. Also, alone time gives you a sense of comfort, which helps you to de-stress. Having a relaxed mind will help in boosting your morale and fighting spirit to take hold of the challenges that you are facing.

47. Learn to Set Aside Time for Relaxation

I cannot emphasize enough how important it is to have the time to relax and unwind each day. Relaxing is great as it enables you to rejuvenate and have the energy to undertake the next day's activities. If you never find time to relax, you will always be tired, and you will lack the energy (and enthusiasm) to undertake various activities.

It is also during your relaxation time that you can evaluate your workday, and think about whether you could have done anything better. This gives you insight on what you need to adjust the following day to have a more productive and organized day.

48. Take Breathers

It is essential to take breathers throughout the day. Our brains are always on the go doing this or the other. It is advisable to take short breaks of five minutes throughout the day, to simply pause, clear your mind, and then get back to work. These breathers are important as they enable you to remain focused, especially when doing lengthy tasks. Remember that we can only concentrate for so long, after which our minds switch off. To fully optimize your performance at work, take breaks.

Chapter 4:
Strategies to Help You Stay Organized

49. Have a Positive Attitude toward Life

Do your plans always go exactly as you thought they would? Most likely they do not. I understand that this can be very frustrating, and that it stresses people out. You need to understand that sometimes things don't always go as expected. Acknowledge this, and things will be much easier. Make it a point to look at the positive side of things. It might be difficult at first, but it is possible.

When you are positive about things that happen to you, you can easily change bleak situations into better situations. Successful people often say, "It's not the problem that is the problem – it's the way you look at the problem." That is how powerful our perception is.

When you adopt positive thinking, you will not become easily depressed. Problems will not hamper your ability to perform and clutter will not be a problem for you. You see challenges as opportunities to learn, to make yourself a better person than yesterday. Doesn't that sound much better?

50. Always Have a Plan B

When your plans take a different turn than expected, it's always a good idea to have a Plan B to get back on track. If you have a back-up plan, you anticipate snags along the way, and whatever happens will not come as a surprise as you will know what to do next.

A back-up plan ensures that, whatever happens, you go right back on track. For instance, if you have set aside the weekend for a major decluttering at home and your folks come over, insisting that you travel with them on a camping trip, why not suggest that you have a backyard barbecue with the neighbors and yard sale instead? That way, you can still do the decluttering and spend time with them, without having to travel. Also, you could sell those things you wish to dispose of at the yard sale! How cool is that?

51. Foresee and Avoid Problems

Just as you wouldn't go out of the house without a coat and an umbrella on a grey day, in the same way, you need to anticipate problems and take the appropriate steps to avoid them or at least mitigate the risk. Take the time to evaluate the different aspects of your life and foresee any problems. This is critical to making sure that nothing ever catches you by surprise.

How can you be in a position to foresee problems? You need to use your sixth sense (or gut feeling, for other people) and spend a few minutes every day to think about your future, the plans you have and what could go wrong. It is through these moments that you can evaluate your life and put things in order. Once you can foresee and avoid potential problems, you will have a better, more organized future since you not only have a Plan B but also a plan C, D, E ... and the list continues.

52. Establish a Reward System

As human beings, we respond better to doing certain tasks when we know that there is a reward upon completion. This also works wonders in your journey to organize your life.

Rather than just assume that you will organize your life because it is in your best interest, why not have a way of rewarding yourself once you organize a certain aspect of your life?

Once your brain registers that there will be a reward for doing something, you will find it much easier to accomplish your goal of staying organized. However, avoid making the reward a no-holds-barred shopping spree, as this will cancel out your decluttering efforts! Why not celebrate by going to a nice place over the weekend, or doing something you love like fishing or hiking?

53. Put Things Back Right Away

I know we are all guilty of taking something from its storage place and failing to return it right away. You tell yourself that you will return such items next time you're cleaning the house. Well, imagine if you say the same thing for over 20 items. By the end of the week, you will have 20 items to replace, which could have been avoided had you returned them after use.

Always have the habit of putting everything back to where it is supposed to be immediately after using it. This will keep an unruly pile from growing all over the house yet again.

54. Eliminate Distractions

Distractions slow down your progress towards organizing your life. You need to reduce distractions as much as possible; a distraction could be as simple as watching your favorite TV show during your decluttering time. What happens? You end up not completing a lot. This distraction will not let you enjoy the full benefits of organizing your life. You may even end up preferring to watch your favorite show instead of tidying up.

Always ensure that you concentrate on one thing at a time, as multitasking makes you lose focus. Eliminate distractions, as they rob you of your time and you end up not accomplishing your targets.

55. Deal with Your Impulses

We all have impulses, whether it is the impulse to buy, eat or watch a movie. While we all have impulses, what separates the successful person from the rest is the actions taken when these impulses occur. It is important to master the art of dealing with your impulses. An effective way of dealing with impulses is to think about how you felt last time you acted on impulse. If you felt guilt, ask yourself if you would want to experience that again.

You can also opt to do something else to take your mind off the temptation. If you have a need to buy something because it is very cheap, try thinking of something else to take your mind off the purchase decision. You may also opt to avoid the impulse altogether if you are finding it hard to deal with it. If you think that switching the TV on makes you just want to watch TV and not do other important things like organizing your house, then don't switch it on. Once you deal with impulses, you will be much more capable of sticking to your plans.

56. Remain Firm in Your Resolve

Deciding to change your life and organize things is a hard and difficult decision to make, as you will need to change many things in order to carry it out. As humans, we tend to be very resistant to change, and at times you may feel that the change is overwhelming.

This is where you need to be firm in your resolve to have a more organized home. Once you start enjoying the benefits of an organized home, no one will need to motivate you to get organized, since you will already know how greatly an organized life benefits you.

57. Remind Yourself of Your Achievements

Sometimes, in order to carry on with the necessary changes in life, we ought to be reminded of the impact that they are having. Trying to change your life without having something to remind you of how far you have come is harmful.

For instance, recovering drug addicts receive a chip or something to remind them of their journey to live a drug-free life. This has to be the same for you. Find something that will remind you of how far you have come, then hold onto it. Each time you feel as if organizing your life is becoming too hard, remember how bad your life was without any sort of organization.

58. Use Productivity or Task Management Apps

With the advancement in technology, you can track almost anything with your smartphone. Embrace technology and make use of productivity and task management apps. These apps are especially helpful if you have a hard time moving from one task to another. You install productivity apps on your smartphone or PC, and they help you keep track of the tasks that you have listed there. Through these apps, you will be able to track the progress of different tasks as well as manage your to-do list appropriately.

59. Understand Opportunity Costs

In business, taking one course of action will definitely prevent the business from taking on another task. This is because of our limited resources, and so we need to use these resources sparingly and wisely.

When you start organizing your life, the greatest problem to deal with is the management of time. To put this into perspective, you need to understand that you cannot do everything and that there will be opportunity costs for doing one task. For instance, if you had planned to organize your office and then you also schedule a night out with friends, choose wisely. You need to understand that time is a limited resource, and if you go out you will push the cleaning to another timeslot, and maybe mess up your entire schedule for a few days. Understand that unscheduled events will interfere with your plans, making it hard for you to organize your life and stick to your schedule.

60. Eat a Balanced Diet Full of Fruits and Vegetables

Eating right is the key to living a healthy and comfortable life. If you are constantly eating junk, you will have no energy to do all the things you aspire to do. This is why it is important that you start eating the right foods now.

You do not want to have a future where you are constantly in the hospital because you are suffering from an illness, and have to spend the money you worked so hard for on medication. Learn to eat foods like whole grains, vegetables and fruits. Such foods will give you the energy you need to do all the tasks that need to be done, and you will not feel tired and out of breath. This is also a great investment for your future, as you are ensuring yourself better health.

61. Stick to What Works

I am sure that you have tried so many things trying to get organized. My advice is to find what works for you and stick to it. If you have the tendency of switching to different organizational strategies (like some people do with fad diets), then you are headed nowhere. If you maintain this behavior, you will be one frustrated person who is always trying everything where nothing seems to work. Actually, instead of organizing your life, you will be in one big mess that you may not even get yourself out of.

My advice is: don't waste your time and money obsessively seeking the best new thing. Before you can say that you have tried something and it has not worked, try to give the strategy some time to work. It could be that the strategy is not suitable to your lifestyle, or because you are resistant to change. Give it some time, say three months. If it really does not work for you, then that is the only time you should switch to another strategy.

62. Review Your Progress

It is so easy to get lost in the midst of all the things we do that we hardly find time to check whether we are actually making progress. As you start your journey to organizing your life, ensure that you set aside some time to review what you have done, and what you have achieved so far. This should highlight what you need to change for greater effectiveness.

63. Practice Minimalism

Minimalism is about taking pleasure in having less stuff. Stuff could be physical, financial or social – anything which keeps your mind so pre-occupied that you never seem to live in the moment.

By embracing minimalism, you derive satisfaction in having fewer things, and you only keep what truly matters. To achieve this, you have to develop a minimalist mindset, which will direct you towards ending your desire to buy more stuff in the hopes that it will give you satisfaction. Minimalism is about unchaining yourself from the slavery of consumerism that has convinced us that buying more is the way to go.

Conclusion

Having a disorganized life can prevent you from enjoying life as you should. Instead, it pushes you to always be in a rush to accomplish different things. Adopting the strategies outlined in this book will help you organize yourself and live a more fulfilling life.

Good luck in your journey of organizing your home, your career, and your life!

Key Takeaways

- You need to be ready to embrace change if you are to organize your life.
- De-cluttering is compulsory if you want to organize yourself and your life. The key is to separate emotions from possessions.
- Having a to-do list and sticking to that schedule is the way to getting organized.
- Stick to what works; don't be too quick to dispute something and say that it does not work.
- Think positively. This makes any challenge much lighter.

How to Put This Information into Action

1. First, you need to ensure that you have a schedule every morning of what you intend to finish over the day.

2. Secondly, you should not buy anything new if you have something that can do the same thing at home. If you have to buy it, then you need to dispose of the other one.

3. Always stick to your plans. This does not mean that you cannot be flexible, but before you make a decision to deviate from you plans, evaluate the situation and determine whether it is important.

4. Finally, ask for help if you feel overwhelmed with all things you need to do. You will be amazed at how people are always willing to help.

Resources for Further Reading

Websites

Zen Habits: http://zenhabits.net/27-great-tips-to-keep-your-life-organized/

Huffington Post: www.huffingtonpost.com/2013/03/20/organize-your-life-life-organization_n_2908774.html

Selfication: http://www.selfication.com/simplify/

Becoming Minimalist: www.becomingminimalist.com/creative-ways-to-declutter/

Life Hack: www.lifehack.org/articles/lifestyle/how-to-declutter-your-life-and-reduce-stress.html

Blogs

Just A Girl And Her Blog: http://justagirlandherblog.com/how-i-organized-my-whole-life/

A Bowl Full of Lemons: http://www.abowlfulloflemons.net/

Modern Parents Messy Kids: www.modernparentsmessykids.com/2012/02/im-woman-with-plan-and-routine-and.html

Clean Mama: http://www.cleanmama.net/category/organizing

Preview of *DIY Cleaning and Organizing: A 21-Day Guide to a Clean and Organized Home*

Cleaning Your Kitchen and Dining Area

Day Five: Surface Cleaning Your Kitchen

The kitchen plays a very vital role, not only in our life but also in our health. An unclean kitchen is a breeding ground for germs and bacteria. It is of vital importance that your kitchen is sparkling clean and disinfected. The primary objective for day five is surface cleaning the kitchen, while the secondary objective is disinfecting.

Primary Objective

Dirty dishes present a bad picture of your kitchen; not only do they make the kitchen look grossly untidy, they produce bad odors. This is due to the growth of bacteria in the food residue that remains on them. An unclean kitchen can cause illnesses such as diarrhea and food poisoning. For this day, wash the dirty dishes, pick up any trash that might be lying around, organize the dishes in their racks and make sure to clean the kitchen sink and the counter tops. The best way to make sure that your dishes are sparkling clean is to wash them with warm soapy water and rinse under clean running water.

Secondary Objective

In order to clean your kitchen effectively, it is essential to disinfect frequently. You can use commercial disinfectant or a homemade one if you are not too enthusiastic about commercial cleaning products. Make sure you disinfect the kitchen sink, counter tops, and any meat cutting boards. To disinfect meat boards, use vinegar or baking soda.

Day 5 Cleaning Tip

Do not let dishes pile up; instead, wash each dish after use and institute the same policy for your family members. This will help you make sure that your kitchen is consistently clean.

Day Six: Deep Cleaning Your Kitchen

The primary objective is to clean every nook and cranny in the kitchen, while the secondary objective is to effectively arrange and store all your kitchenware.

Primary Objective

Start by cleaning the sinks with vinegar and baking soda, then scrub the stove with ammonia to remove the burn marks and food residue. To clean and disinfect your kitchen sink, use vinegar, baking soda, rock salt and lemon or ice cubes. Clean behind the stove, at the back of the cabinets and shelves, and all the other spots that you normally don't get to clean while performing a quick clean. To clean your greasy oven, you can use a mixture of dishwashing soap, baking soda and vinegar. To clean your microwave and remove food stuck to it, use one tablespoon of vinegar and one cup of water and heat it in the microwave for about five minutes. To clean your coffee maker, run water and vinegar through it. Make sure to clean behind the oven, fridge and cabinets, as well as dusting in all the places that you do not normally dust. You may have to move many of the items in your kitchen to access out-of-the-way places. Don't worry, after you do this once you won't have to deep clean your kitchen constantly.

Secondary Objective

Store all your kitchenware correctly; you may want to have a designated cabinet or place for keeping spoons, plates, pots and cups. Since the cabinets are now sparkling clean, the pots will be protected from dust.

Day 6 Cleaning Tip

Always make sure that you have vinegar and baking soda in the house since they have many uses in cleaning your home.

Day Seven: Cleaning Your Dining Area

We are now at day seven. I am sure that you can look around your house and see the progress that we have achieved so far. On day seven, we will again have two objectives: the primary objective is to surface and deep clean your dining area, while the secondary objective will be to polish all your cutlery and dining ware.

Primary Objective

Start by picking up any food residue (leftovers) that might be in the dining area and clean the plates or utensils. Secondly, wipe all the chairs if they are wooden; if they have any cushions, you can take them out to the patio and pat them with a wooden stick. If your dinner table is wooden, you can also polish it. Remember to clean the table legs. Arrange the table and chairs properly.

Secondary Objective

Although polishing the cutlery and dining ware might take a while, the short time you took to clean the dining area should leave enough time for the polishing. Using a clean kitchen towel, wipe down your cutlery to achieve a smooth sheen. The best way to achieve this is by cleaning the silverware in a mixture of water and baking soda and then air-drying them. You can be sure that the silverware will sparkle when you wipe it with a soft towel after having washed it in a mixture of water and baking soda.

Day 7 Cleaning Tip

To make sure that no other rooms harbor food residue that attracts insects, ensure that you take your meals only in the dining area.

Download DIY Cleaning and Organizing: A 21 Day Guide to a Clean and Organized Home.

More Books You Might Like

House Cleaning Secrets: A Quick and Easy 7-Day Cleaning Course to Help Organize, Declutter and Keep Your Home Looking Effortlessly Spotless

Minimalist Organization: A Modern Minimalist's Guide to Organizing Your Home and Keeping it Effortlessly Spotless

Household DIY: Save Time and Money with Do It Yourself Hints & Tips on Furniture, Clothes, Pests, Stains, Residues, Odors and More!

Essential Oils: Essential Oils & Aromatherapy for Beginners: Proven Secrets to Weight Loss, Skin Care, Hair Care & Stress Relief Using Essential Oil Recipes

Apple Cider Vinegar for Beginners: An Apple Cider Vinegar Handbook with Proven Secrets to Natural Weight Loss, Optimum Health and Beautiful Skin

Body Butter Recipes: Proven Formula Secrets to Making All Natural Body Butters that Will Hydrate and Rejuvenate Your Skin

Homemade Body Scrubs and Masks for Beginners: Over 60 All-Natural Quick & Easy Recipes for Body & Facial Masks to Help Exfoliate, Nourish & Provide the Ultimate Care for Your Skin

Natural Remedies that Work: How to Heal and Protect Yourself without the Use of Prescriptions

For even more books that could help you, please check out the following link:

http://amzn.to/1svIfaN

Your Free Bonus

As a way of thanking you for your purchase, I'm offering you an opportunity to sign up and be a part of an exclusive book list where members get advanced notice on high-quality books.

To be part of this exclusive club, click on the link below:

https://docs.google.com/forms/d/1ttDqtdRjOeAEtA-BKnq5Hw668vjQSoVWcXCGQ8z9frA/viewform

www.ingramcontent.com/pod-product-compliance
Lightning Source LLC
Chambersburg PA
CBHW070029030426
42335CB00017B/2360